366 Tips
For a
Successful Job
Search

Other titles from Rosstrum Publishing

Fast Track for Caregivers

Lawless in Brazil

Watch for these future volumes

Timberline

366 Tips
For a
Successful Job
Search

by

Cynthia Wright

Rosstrum Publishing
Nashua, New Hampshire

Rosstrum Publishing books are available at discounts when purchased in bulk for premiums and sales promotions as well as for fundraising or educational use. Based on quantities, special editions can be created to specification. For details, contact the publisher by mail or by e-mail.

Rosstrum Publishing
8 Strawberry Bank Road
Suite 20
Nashua, NH 03062-2763
RosstrumPublishing@gmail.com
www.RosstrumPublishing.com

Library of Congress Control Number: 2009926792

Manufactured in the United States of America
First printing June 2009
1 3 5 7 9 10 8 6 4 2

To my Mother
Who always knew I had the Wright Stuff

Acknowledgements

I owe many thanks to those who helped me with this book.

I cannot offer enough thanks to those who served as readers, offering both criticism and encouragement. Robert J. Lepecki, Kforce Professional Staffing, Burlington, MA; Maria Matarazzo, Chair of the Division of Business Administration, Rivier College, Nashua, NH; Pamela Wilkie, Talent Acquisition Specialist, Andover, MA; Charles Campbell, Argyle Consultants, Holliston, MA; Chuck Tewell, Lockheed-Martin, Chelmsford, MA; and Lynn Rapa, City of Salem, Salem, NH.

Thanks also to my editor and publisher, Joe Ross of Rosstrum Publications, who drove me crazy with changes and suggestions.

Cynthia Wright

Introduction

When the idea for this book/perpetual calendar started coming together, the unemployment rate in the United States was 4.02%. Since then, the unemployment rate has doubled, with no end in sight.

This book/perpetual calendar can help everyone in a job search, from the college graduate venturing out into the work force for the first time, to the career changers who have become disenchanted with their present careers.

As a recruiter and professional interviewer for more than 16 years, several things have become evident. Despite the influx of career-related information, candidates still do not know how to interview, network, or look for a job.

The hope is that this work can help the new graduate, the career changer, the candidate re-entering the workforce, the person transitioning from the military, and anyone else who is looking for a new job, another job, or a new career.

If one of these 366 tips helps someone land a job, the book *did* its job! Enjoy.

Cynthia Wright
The Wright Stuff

A word about Holidays

Many holidays fall on a day of the week rather than on a specific day. Some of those are indicated here.

January, 3rd Monday; Martin Luther King Day
February, 3rd Monday; President's Day
March, 2nd Sunday; Daylight Savings starts
May, 2nd Sunday; Mother's Day
May, 3rd Saturday; Armed Forces Day
May, last Monday; Memorial Day
June, 3rd Sunday; Father's Day
July, 4th Sunday; Parents' Day
September, 1st Monday; Labor Day
October, 2nd Monday; Columbus Day
November, 1st Sunday; Daylight Savings ends
November, 4th Thursday; Thanksgiving

January 1
New Year's Day

If you are unhappy in your current job, look for another one.

My notes:

January 2

Even if you hate your job, it is important to continue to do your work and to do it well while searching for a new position.

My notes:

January 3

If a job is causing you to become burnt-out or stresssed-out, look for another job.

My notes:

January 4

When **you're** stressed, you

care too much.

My notes:

January 5

When you're burned out, you

do not see any hope of

improvement.

My notes:

January 6

Most burnout has to do with

the workplace.

My notes:

January 7

Those most at risk for stress or burnout may be service professionals who spend time attending to the needs of others.

My notes:

January 8

If you are being abused at work, notify your manager or supervisor.

My notes:

January 9

If you are being abused at work, notify Human Resources.

My notes:

January 10

If you are being abused at work, you may want to consult with an employment lawyer.

My notes:

January 11

If you are being abused at

work, find another job.

My notes:

January 12

If you need help, use your company's EAP (Employee Assistance Programs) which are usually free and confidential.

My notes:

January 13

Some companies may offer unpaid leaves of absence to enable employees to resolve their problems.

My notes:

January 14

Do not slack off because you

feel that a great new job is

around the corner.

My notes:

January 15

When looking for a new job, do it on your own time. IT departments monitor employees computer time and can tell if you are doing non-company work on company time.

My notes:

January 16

When necessary, take

several vacation days to net-

work, update your resume, and

participate in interviews.

My notes:

January 17

You must learn to effectively manage your own career. If you don't do it, nobody else will.

My notes:

January 18

Changing jobs may become necessary. Taking smaller steps rather than doing everything at once makes the process simple, less frightening, and most of all, attainable.

My notes:

January 19

Keep all working relationships on a positive, professional, and friendly note. Remember, you want to leave when you are ready to leave and not when the company says, "You're fired."

My notes:

January 20

Don't burn bridges, whether

changing jobs by choice or by

being laid off.

My notes:

January 21

If you are laid off, make sure

you have enough money to live

comfortably for nine months.

My notes:

January 22

If you are laid off, file for unemployment benefits as soon as possible.

My notes:

January 23

Getting laid off not a stigma.

Let *everyone* know that you are looking for a job. This is called networking.

My notes:

January 24

If you are laid off, secure insurance, either from your spouse, COBRA, Medicaid, or privately.

My notes:

January 25

Explain to your family that you may have to live on less while you conduct a proper job search.

My notes:

January 26

If you are laid off, act quickly to secure all your benefits including sick leave, unused vacation, personal days and severance pay.

My notes:

January 27

If you are laid off, immediately review your retirement plans for rollover possibilities or conversion from a 401(k) plan to an IRA.

My notes:

January 28

If you are in financial trouble,

think before you act.

My notes:

January 29

Figure out ways to cut expenses while you conduct your job search.

My notes:

January 30

Maintain a healthy balance with your job search and family life. You will be more focused and your family life will not suffer as much.

My notes:

January 31

Make time during the job search process to go out and have fun as a family.

My notes:

February 1

Exercise. It gets your heart pumping and releases endor-phins which make you feel better.

My notes:

February 2
Groundhog Day

Take additional courses to make yourself more marketable for your next job.

My notes:

February 3

Buy books on topics that you are rusty on and which relate to your field and read them.

My notes:

February 4

Many adult education programs offer courses that are not expensive.

My notes:

February 5

**K**eep your expectations at a

realistic and reasonable level.

My notes:

February 6

Commit to specific job search goals each week.

My notes:

February 7

Searching for a job *is* a full-time job. Therefore, get up at the same time each day.

My notes:

February 8

Limit TV watching until the

evening hours. Your full-time job

is to find a job.

My notes:

February 9

Recognize that searching for a job is one of the most stressful things that you can go through.

My notes:

February 10

Be positive and realistic.

My notes:

February 11

Remember, you are only being judged on one facet of who you are as it relates to the job you are interviewing for.

My notes:

February 12
Lincoln's Birthday

Ask people closest to you if

they sense negative vibes.

Often, we do not realize how we

come across to others.

My notes:

February 13

Be aware of the steps involved in a comprehensive job search.

My notes:

February 14
St. Valentine's Day

Focus on what is positive in

life instead of what is negative.

My notes:

February 15

Combat and avoid the negative feelings that are part of a job search.

My notes:

February 16

Do not cause unnecessary

stress and aggravation to your

family by being negative.

My notes:

February 17

Do not let a negative attitude

hurt your job search progress.

My notes:

February 18

Do not let a negative attitude adversely affect other parts of your life.

My notes:

February 19

Do not let a negative attitude

cause you to ignore career

avenues that may otherwise

prove fruitful.

My notes:

February 20

Do not let a negative attitude

distort your point of view.

My notes:

February 21

Do not allow a negative attitude to make you feel tired and worn out.

My notes:

February 22
Washington's Birthday

Do not let a negative attitude

destroy your feelings of

confidence.

My notes:

February 23

Do not let a negative attitude destroy your feelings of self-worth.

My notes:

February 24

Be proactive in your job search. Never wait by the phone.

My notes:

February 25

Involve everyone in the job search process. This makes the task much easier.

My notes:

February 26

Ask your parents, relatives,

and friends for job leads.

My notes:

February 27

Consider industries that you

may not have considered as a

way to expand your network.

My notes:

February 28

Research hospital and

healthcare-related openings.

My notes:

February 29
Leap Day

Research positions at

colleges and universities.

My notes:

March 1

Research government

positions.

My notes:

March 2

Consider non-traditional careers. A non-traditional career is one where 75% or more of the workers are of the opposite gender.

My notes:

March 3

The biggest positive of working in a non-traditional career is the benefit of following your dreams and the satisfaction that comes from the empowerment of a job done well.

My notes:

March 4

People in non-traditional jobs

will receive more attention.

My notes:

March 5

A positive aspect of non-traditional careers for women is that the pay is typically much higher in careers where men dominate.

My notes:

March 6

For men, a positive of a non-traditional career is that you are often given positions of responsibility sooner.

My notes:

March 7

A negative for non-traditional careers is the lack of mentors.

My notes:

March 8

A negative in non-traditional careers is the disapproving feelings from co-workers, especially for female workers in traditionally male careers.

My notes:

March 9

A negative aspect of a non-traditional career is that you may receive little or no support from family and friends who may question your motives.

My notes:

March 10

Women may find the physical challenges of some non-traditional careers over-whelming.

My notes:

March 11

Consider turning your hobby

into a successful business.

My notes:

March 12

To turn a hobby into a

successful business, you need

to have a plan.

My notes:

March 13

Before turning your hobby

into a successful business,

research the prospects for

success.

My notes:

March 14

Ask an expert how to turn your hobby into a successful business.

My notes:

March 15

Don't get involved with a company that does not make the nature of its business clear to you up front.

My notes:

March 16

If you feel you have found a genuine work-at-home oppor-tunity, check it out thoroughly.

My notes:

March 17
St. Patrick's Day

If a work-at-home opportunity

requires money up front, do not

send it.

My notes:

March 18

**If** you feel that you have been

scammed, call your state's

Attorney General's office.

My notes:

March 19

Use *www.fraud.org* to find out

if a work-at-home opportunity

has criminal complaints lodged

against it.

My notes:

March 20

Use *www.fraud.org* to find out

if the work-at-home company

has engaged in illegal business

practices.

My notes:

March 21

If a work-at home opportunity promises that you can work your own hours, it might be a scam.

My notes:

March 22

If a work at home opportunity states "unlimited earning potential," it might be a scam.

My notes:

March 23

Research all work-at-home

opportunities using The Better

Business Bureau

(*www.bbb.org*), your state's

Attorney General's office, or

www.fraud.com.

My notes:

March 24

Never share your bank account, credit card information, or social security number with a prospective employer. Scammers use this information to steal from you.

My notes:

March 25

There is always competition

for good positions.

My notes:

March 26

Stay away from a company that wants to hire you immediately without an interview.

My notes:

March 27

Set performance goals, meet

or exceed them, and use them

as additional important tools

when you start your interview

process.

My notes:

March 28

Write your goals down.

My notes:

March 29

When setting goals, think of the end result first.

My notes:

March 30

Focus on one goal at a time.

For instance, if your goal is to

get a job, focus on that goal.

My notes:

March 31

Organize your job search. It gives you a solid road map to follow.

My notes:

April 1
April Fool's Day

Establish a weekly plan;

follow it consistently and

conscientiously. The strong

feeling of accomplishment will

create positive feelings and a

higher level of confidence.

My notes:

April 2

Be prepared to be judged on your strengths and your weaknesses.

My notes:

April 3

You will be judged on your appearance.

My notes:

April 4

Be prepared. You will be

judged on your personality.

My notes:

April 5

Don't expect to always be

liked and appreciated during

your job search.

My notes:

April 6

Focus your thoughts on prior successes.

My notes:

April 7

Keep a positive attitude.

My notes:

April 8

Be aware of how others perceive you.

My notes:

April 9

Join a job-seeker support group. This can provide a forum to vent and share feelings with others.

My notes:

April 10

To avoid the hurt associated with being judged, talk to someone you trust about your concerns, fears, and thoughts.

My notes:

April 11

The best way to get an edge on the competition is to make yourself a more competitive candidate.

My notes:

April 12

Don't be shy about sharing
your background and accomplishments during an interview.
It's an excellent way to market
yourself.

My notes:

April 13

Some weeks will be busy with activity and job offers. Other weeks will be slow.

My notes:

April 14

Show interest in others by

listening to them.

My notes:

April 15
Income Tax Deadline

Listening is power.

My notes:

April 16

When you're talking, you're not giving yourself the chance to learn anything.

My notes:

April 17

Be a good listener. A good listener asks questions in a non-threatening manner.

My notes:

April 18

Show interest in the person

and demonstrate a genuine

willingness to listen.

My notes:

April 19

Be a good listener by using eye contact.

My notes:

April 20

Be a good listener. A good

listener does not interrupt the

speaker.

My notes:

April 21

A good listener is aware of the speaker's verbal and non-verbal behavior.

My notes:

April 22

Try to understand the

speaker's point-of-view.

My notes:

April 23

Be a good listener. Respond to the speaker in a constructive and positive manner.

My notes:

April 24

A good listener is open-

minded and pays attention.

My notes:

April 25

Try to listen 75% of the time

and talk 25% of the time.

My notes:

April 26

Go to all social functions regardless of whether or not others in your field will be there. You never know who you will meet.

My notes:

April 27

When socializing, it's better to say nothing than to do all of the talking.

My notes:

April 28

Always carry business cards

and resumes that include your

contact information.

My notes:

CYNTHIA WRIGHT

April 29

Make a list of significant

accomplishments.

My notes:

April 30

 **Attend Chamber of Com-**

merce meetings as a way to

network.

My notes:

May 1

Attend trade association

events as a way to network.

My notes:

May 2

Get enough rest. If you are

tired, you will not have the

energy to network.

My notes:

May 3

Use networking sites such as *LinkedIn* to network.

My notes:

May 4

Use blogs as networking tools.

My notes:

May 5
Cinco de Mayo

Use networking sites such as

Facebook to network.

My notes:

May 6

Be careful about what you

post on social networking sites.

Employers may use these sites

to find out more about you.

My notes:

May 7

Do not establish a user name

on a social network site which

may offend a prospective

employer.

My notes:

May 8

Network with family, friends, neighbors, acquaintances, past colleagues, and former teachers (especially if you are a recent graduate).

My notes:

May 9

Network in church, at the

gym, and at trade shows.

My notes:

May 10

Network at clubs you belong to.

My notes:

May 11

Network at organizations you belong to.

My notes:

May 12

Consider industries that you

may have not considered as a

way to expand your network.

My notes:

May 13

Attend college alumni events.

My notes:

May 14

After hours company events

are a great way to network.

My notes:

May 15

After hours company events are an excellent way to learn what's going on in your organization or company.

My notes:

May 16

The relaxed atmosphere of a local watering hole gives you the chance to network with co-workers and executives.

My notes:

May 17

Just because alcohol is

served at happy hours or

company functions does not

mean you have to drink.

My notes:

May 18

Do not jeopardize your

employment by over-drinking

and acting unprofessionally.

My notes:

May 19

When you are at an after hours work event, don't forget that even though you are out of the office, you are still with colleagues, managers, and executives.

My notes:

May 20

At a company function, carry a non-alcoholic beverage to avoid drinking too much.

My notes:

May 21

It's better to show up, have a drink and some food, stay for an hour and leave, than to not show up at all.

My notes:

May 22

At a company function, do not

say anything that will embarrass

you. There is nothing worse

than embarrassing yourself and

having it become office gossip

on Monday morning.

My notes:

May 23

At a company function, let your colleagues get to know you a little better.

My notes:

May 24

on't drink heavily at

company functions.

My notes:

May 25
Memorial Day (actual)

Put yourself in situations that

will increase your chances of

success.

My notes:

May 26

Most jobs are not advertised.

Use networking to find out about

unadvertised jobs.

My notes:

May 27

Use your college career

center to help you with your job

search.

My notes:

May 28

Use the career center

counselors to help you with your

resume.

My notes:

May 29

Use the career center coun-

selors to teach you interviewing

strategies.

My notes:

May 30

Use the career center for job leads.

My notes:

May 31

Contact companies you worked for previously, especially if you left on good terms. They may have jobs.

My notes:

June 1

Most jobs are not advertised.

Use networking to find out about

unadvertised jobs.

My notes:

June 2

Talk to other people. 75% to 80% of all positions are found through networking.

My notes:

June 3

Network all the time. Only 20%-25% of positions are found through the Internet, job fairs, employment agencies, and newspapers.

My notes:

June 4

Search professional organizations' web sites for job postings. Organizations are an excellent way to network.

My notes:

June 5

Post your resume on professional associations' web sites whenever possible. These services are often free of charge.

My notes:

June 6

Look for networking groups that cater to a specific industry or discipline.

My notes:

June 7

In *any* economy, employers usually interview three or more candidates.

My notes:

June 8

Chances are that you will not be the only candidate being interviewed for a job. This is true even if a company takes the first step to recruit you.

My notes:

June 9

When responding to a job posting, include the same "buzz words" that appear on the job posting.

My notes:

June 10

A cover letter should be no

more than one page.

My notes:

June 11

A cover letter should include

your relevant skills.

My notes:

June 12

Address your cover letter to a person instead of "Dear Sir or Madam." If necessary, call the company and ask who the appropriate person is.

My notes:

June 13

Check the spelling of the person's name *twice* when writing a cover letter.

My notes:

June 14
Flag Day

A resume is a marketing

document.

My notes:

June 15

Use a resume to market your skills and talents to a prospective employer.

My notes:

June 16

When creating a resume, use a Times New Roman or Arial 11 point font.

My notes:

June 17

A two or even a three page resume is acceptable. Years of experience cannot fit onto one page.

My notes:

June 18

Check your resume at least twice for misspellings and typographical errors. Have others check your resume for you.

My notes:

June 19

Don't lie on your resume.

Background checks are often

done by an independent

company to verify past

employment, education, criminal

history, credit history, and, if

applicable, driving records.

June 20

Avoid using personal pronouns on your resume, such as *I, me*, and *my*.

My notes:

June 21

Always include specific accomplishments and core competencies on your resume.

My notes:

June 22

Include both paid and unpaid college co-op positions and internships on your resume.

My notes:

June 23

Include all academic honors

on your resume.

My notes:

June 24

Include volunteer jobs on your resume.

My notes:

June 25

Include leadership roles on your resume.

My notes:

June 26

If you mentored an individual, include that on a resume.

My notes:

June 27

Make sure a prospective

employer has at least two ways

to contact you. An e-mail

address and a cell phone

number are appropriate.

My notes:

June 28

Be sure your e-mail address does not give employers the wrong impression. If necessary, establish a new e-mail address for your job search.

My notes:

June 29

Use a chronological resume if you have no gaps in employment.

My notes:

June 30

List your jobs in reverse order on a chronological resume. Your most recent job goes first.

My notes:

July 1

Always put dates of em-

ployment on a resume.

My notes:

July 2

Use a functional resume if you have significant gaps or short employment stints.

My notes:

July 3

Use an objective statement

on your resume to tell prospec-

tive employers what you *want* to

do.

My notes:

July 4
Independence Day

Use a summary statement on your resume to tell a prospective employer what you *are capable* of doing.

My notes:

July 5

Select your references carefully.

My notes:

July 6

Be sure to ask your refer-

ences if it is all right to use

them. Ask *before* you give them

to a prospective employer.

My notes:

July 7

Never put references on a

resume. If employers are

interested in hiring you, they will

ask for them.

My notes:

July 8

When reference checks are done by a company, the questions asked are related to job performance.

My notes:

July 9

When providing references to a company, give at least three professional references.

My notes:

July 10

Judge the effectiveness of your resume by the number of responses you receive.

My notes:

July 11

If you send out 15 resumes and get three responses, you are doing well.

My notes:

July 12

If you send out 100 resumes and get one response, rewrite your resume. Get professional assistance if necessary.

My notes:

July 13

Provide specific examples of how your efforts helped an organization.

My notes:

July 14

If you streamlined a process,

put it on your resume.

My notes:

July 15

If you saved a company

money, put it on your resume.

My notes:

July 16

If you finished a project under

budget, put it on your resume.

My notes:

July 17

When stating your respon-

sibilities on your resume, use

action verbs such as *coordinate,*

create, organize, to better

accentuate your skills and

abilities.

My notes:

July 18

Deal with any negatives on your resume, such as gaps, openly and honestly.

My notes:

July 19

If you are asked about gaps on your resume during an interview, keep your answers simple. Explain that you had to take care of some things and you are excited about the next opportunity.

July 20

Use a dollar amount or percentage to indicate what you did to make your current (or previous) company more profitable or efficient.

My notes:

July 21

The best candidate does not always get the job. The job goes to the candidate that not only has the skills, but interviews well.

My notes:

July 22

Do not sound angry. Anger will come across during an interview.

My notes:

July 23

Be aware of your attitude.

Awareness is the first step in

reversing a poor attitude.

My notes:

July 24

Ask friends and family for an

objective opinion of your

attitude.

My notes:

July 25

Use job fairs to network,

since you will have the oppor-

tunity to meet many employers

face-to-face.

My notes:

CYNTHIA WRIGHT

July 26

Attend college sponsored job fairs. Companies recruit at job fairs.

My notes:

July 27

Get business cards from company representatives attending the job fair.

My notes:

July 28

Research the companies that will be at the job fair.

My notes:

July 29

Use a company's web site to see what they do.

My notes:

July 30

Use a company's web site to find out what jobs are available.

My notes:

July 31

Use a company's web site to find out how the company is doing financially.

My notes:

August 1

Send thank you notes to everyone you speak to at a job fair.

My notes:

August 2

When you meet people at a job fair, you are interviewing, so act and dress professionally.

My notes:

August 3

You will meet many company representatives at job fairs, so bring plenty of neatly stapled copies of your resume.

My notes:

August 4

If you cannot go to the job fair, e-mail your resume to the job fair sponsor and ask that it be forwarded to the attendees.

My notes:

August 5

When you tell someone

about your accomplishments,

practice your speech in front of

a mirror or with friends.

My notes:

August 6

Briefly tell everyone who you are, what you do, your work history, successes, professional strengths, and unique characteristics.

My notes:

CYNTHIA WRIGHT

August 7

Explain what type of job you are looking for.

My notes:

August 8

Select an employment agency that specializes in your field or in the field you are trying to enter.

My notes:

August 9

If an employment agency asks you for money before they help you with a job search, do not pay it. Find another agency.

My notes:

August 10

Do not pay an agency fee.

They are paid by client

companies.

My notes:

August 11

If you feel you've been swindled, call your state's Attorney General's office and the Better Business Bureau (*www.bbb.org*).

My notes:

August 12

When interviewing with an employment agency, have extra resumes with you.

My notes:

August 13

When interviewing with an employment agency, dress professionally.

My notes:

August 14

Arrive ten minutes early for an interview with an employment agency.

My notes:

August 15

Treat the recruiter from an employment agency as you would a prospective employer and act courteously and professionally.

My notes:

August 16

Statistically, only 5%-7% of all jobs are found through employment agencies, so spend 5%-7% of your job search time using them.

My notes:

August 17

A Recruiter is a gatekeeper and often the initial contact you will have with a potential employer.

My notes:

August 18

A Recruiter is an important

part of the interviewing process.

My notes:

August 19

A Recruiter's job is to help you navigate through the interview process.

My notes:

August 20

A Recruiter creates a job description that gets posted both externally and internally within a company.

My notes:

August 21

A Recruiter is the one who decides whether or not your resume gets to the Hiring Manager.

My notes:

August 22

Make sure your resume matches the job description the Recruiter created. The recruiter does the initial screening *out* of resumes.

My notes:

August 23

Recruiters are not career coaches or mentors.

My notes:

August 24

The Recruiter may give you an interview schedule or itinerary with the names of the Hiring Managers, their titles, and how long each interview will last.

My notes:

August 25

A Recruiter may arrange lunch and any kind of travel that may be necessary if you are traveling from out of state.

My notes:

August 26

Recruiters are not in a position to give you the inside scoop on other candidates.

My notes:

August 27

A Recruiter is not in a position to tell you what the Hiring Manager is like.

My notes:

August 28

A recruiter is not going to tell you what to say or not to say during the interview.

My notes:

August 29

A Recruiter's job is not to be your advocate.

My notes:

August 30

A Recruiter is judged on how many qualified candidates are brought into an organization in a cost effective, timely matter.

My notes:

August 31

Impress the Recruiters. They are an important part of an organization, and their feedback on you as a candidate is crucial.

My notes:

September 1

A Recruiter can be one of your best allies in your job search process.

My notes:

September 2

Be friendly with a Recruiter,

but not overly casual or familiar.

My notes:

September 3

Keep personal comments,

jokes, or innuendo to a

minimum.

My notes:

September 4

Do not say or do anything in front of a Recruiter that you would not say or do in front of the prospective employer (or your mother).

My notes:

September 5

Ask the Recruiter, "What kinds of qualities would the ideal candidate have?"

My notes:

September 6

An excellent interview question to pose to a Recruiter is, "How many candidates are you interviewing?"

My notes:

September 7

An excellent interview

question for a Recruiter is,

"When will a hiring decision be

made?"

My notes:

September 8

Ask a Recruiter, "What is the next step in the process?"

My notes:

September 9

Before an interview, research the company using the Internet or Dun and Bradstreet. Learn about their financial status and products and services.

My notes:

September 10

As a candidate, your main objective during a telephone interview is to get asked to come in for an in person interview.

My notes:

September 11
World Trade Center
Terrorist Attack Remembrance

Select a quiet place with no distractions to engage in a telephone interview. Make sure the kids and pets are in another room.

My notes:

September 12

If you are invited for an interview and you are not interested in the position, take the interview. You may be pleasantly surprised and practice makes perfect.

My notes:

September 13

Be articulate and alert during a telephone interview so you will not be screened out.

My notes:

September 14

If you are asked, "Tell me how you handled an irate customer," include details about how you brought the situation to a successful conclusion.

My notes:

September 15

Write down six job-related

questions and bring them to the

interview.

My notes:

September 16
Stepfamily Day

Take a test drive a day or two

before your interview to ensure

you know your destination.

My notes:

September 17
Citizenship Day
Constitution Day

Prepare yourself before an interview.

My notes:

CYNTHIA WRIGHT

September 18

Always get a job description

prior to the interview.

My notes:

September 19

If the recruiter does not supply a job description, search the company's web site for one.

My notes:

September 20

Take control of an interview by being prepared to ask intelligent, insightful job-related questions.

My notes:

September 21

If necessary, practice shaking hands. A firm handshake is important.

My notes:

September 22

Run your hands under warm water to remove the clamminess.

My notes:

September 23

When interviewing, arrive ten

minutes early to gather your

thoughts and relax.

My notes:

September 24

Always bring extra copies of

your resume to a job interview.

My notes:

September 25

You only have one chance to

make a great first impression.

Don't blow it.

My notes:

September 26

The expression, "Clothes make the man (or woman)" is true. If you want to be the VP of Sales, dress like one.

My notes:

September 27

Avoid loud clothes.

My notes:

September 28

Avoid heavy make-up.

My notes:

September 29

Avoid wearing heavy perfume.

My notes:

September 30

Keep jewelry simple.

My notes:

October 1

Business attire is the rule.

However, if you are interviewing

for a position in the trades,

business casual attire is

appropriate.

My notes:

October 2

Approach every interview as if you are the long shot candidate.

My notes:

October 3

Allow give and take when interviewing. An interview is a conversation between two or more people.

My notes:

October 4

Allow every other person equal time to speak.

My notes:

October 5

An informational interview is used to investigate careers you are interested in. Treat it as a traditional interview.

My notes:

October 6

Interview the Recruiter or

Hiring Manager as well as

having them interview you.

My notes:

October 7

Save your questions about specific job requirements and technical details of the job for the Hiring Managers.

My notes:

October 8

Think of an interview as a meeting. This will level the playing field and put things in a proper perspective.

My notes:

October 9

Look forward to the "meeting"

with the same sense of

anticipation as you would if you

were meeting a friend for lunch.

This will take some of the

pressure off and make it a more

pleasant experience.

October 10

Remember, if you being interviewed, the interviewer potentially wants to hire you.

My notes:

October 11

Use an informational interview to network, since it gives you the opportunity to talk to people who can help you.

My notes:

October 12

Make eye contact with the individuals interviewing you.

My notes:

October 13

Trust your intuition.

My notes:

October 14

Ask questions that are job

related.

My notes:

October 15

Do not ask non job-related

questions.

My notes:

October 16
Boss's Day

Ask why the position became available.

My notes:

October 17

Ask what qualities the ideal candidate would have.

My notes:

October 18

Ask when a hiring decision will be made.

My notes:

October 19

During an interview, ask about job-related travel.

My notes:

October 20

During an interview, ask about advancement oppor-tunities.

My notes:

October 21

During an interview, ask where the department falls in the corporate structure.

My notes:

October 22

At the interview, ask who you will report to and what position they hold.

My notes:

October 23

At the interview, ask if you will be on call and, if so, what the hours are.

My notes:

October 24

Do not ask questions about

benefits.

My notes:

October 25

Do not ask questions about

vacation time.

My notes:

October 26

Save questions about benefits and vacation time until after you are offered the job.

My notes:

October 27

Do not be intimidated by a group or panel interview. It is used to save time.

My notes:

October 28

During a group interview, make eye contact not only with the individual who asked the question, but with others in the group.

My notes:

October 29

Do not do anything that will

distract the interviewer.

Research has shown that 90%

of all communication is non-

verbal.

My notes:

October 30

Mirror the body language of the person who is interviewing you.

My notes:

October 31
Halloween

Maintain good posture. It shows the interviewer that you are confident and competent.

My notes:

November 1

Before answering a question, take a breath and think for a moment.

My notes:

November 2

Breathe slowly. It will give you

a few seconds to get your

thoughts together.

My notes:

November 3

Answer interview questions in

a strong, positive tone of voice.

My notes:

November 4

Interviewers are actively listening even if they stop taking notes.

My notes:

November 5

Discuss only job-related topics during an interview.

My notes:

November 6

Do not say negative things

about a past employer or

manager.

My notes:

November 7

Do not say bad things about a current manager during an interview.

My notes:

November 8

Do not say bad things about your current employer during an interview.

My notes:

November 9

Be honest and open about your accomplishments.

My notes:

November 10

Don't overemphasize your roles and responsibilities. It could come back to haunt you.

My notes:

November 11
Veteran's Day

Your goal when leaving an interview is to learn what you need to know in order to make an intelligent career decision.

My notes:

November 12

Ask each person you inter-

view with for a business card.

My notes:

November 13

After each interview, thank

the interviewers for their time.

My notes:

November 14

After every interview, send a thank you note to each interviewer. Their contact information will be on the business cards.

My notes:

November 15

Customize each thank you note, and review key points from the interview.

My notes:

November 16

You may use e-mailed thank you notes.

My notes:

November 17

Thank you notes should

include a thank you for the

interviewer's time.

My notes:

November 18

Thank you notes should summarize your skills.

My notes:

November 19

Thank you notes should include your continued interest in the position.

My notes:

November 20

Follow-up is important. E-mail

or call the hiring manager one

week after your interview.

My notes:

November 21

Stand out. Follow-up rein-

forces the idea that you are still

interested in the position.

My notes:

November 22

Do not assume you will be

offered a position because you

were referred by an employee.

My notes:

November 23

Do not assume you will be

offered a position because you

once worked for the company.

My notes:

November 24

A prospective employer may use pre-employment tests to determine if you have a high probability of success in a particular area.

My notes:

November 25

A pre-employment test can tell a Sales Manager if you have the ability to qualify a good prospect, negotiate, up sell, and close a deal.

My notes:

November 26

A prospective employer may use a personality and motivation test to measure your pattern of thinking, feeling, and behaving.

My notes:

November 27

A prospective employer may use a pre-employment test to assess your level of drive and motivation.

My notes:

November 28

A prospective employer may use a pre-employment test to measure intelligence or mental ability, and your aptitude and ability to quickly acquire job knowledge.

My notes:

November 29

A prospective employer may use a pre-employment test to measure integrity which may identify job applicants who are likely to lie, steal, or use illegal substances.

My notes:

November 30

A prospective employer may use a pre-employment test to assess basic literacy and/or math skills.

My notes:

December 1

A prospective employer may administer psychological testing.

My notes:

December 2

A prospective employer may require a pre-employment drug test as a condition of employment.

My notes:

December 3

A prospective employer may test applicants on specific job skills.

My notes:

December 4

If a company wants to administer pre-employment tests, they must comply with the Equal Employment Opportunity Commission (EEOC) and Americans with Disabilities Act (ADA) regulations.

December 5

A pre-employment test must be job-related.

My notes:

December 6

A pre-employment test cannot adversely impact a specific group of people.

My notes:

December 7
Pearl Harbor Day

If you are a person with disabilities, a pre-employment test cannot pose any hardship related to your disability.

My notes:

December 8

There is no right or wrong answer on some pre-employ-ment tests.

My notes:

December 9

Answer all questions on any

pre-employment test openly and

honestly.

My notes:

December 10

Some tests will ask the same questions many different ways, to see if you are consistent in your answers.

My notes:

December 11

When taking a pre-

employment test, relax.

My notes:

December 12

Remember that job offers are

negotiable most of the time.

My notes:

December 13

Your strongest negotiating position is just after you are offered a position and just before you accept that offer.

My notes:

December 14

When you receive a job offer, know the appropriate salary range. Use *www.salary.com*, *www.monster.com*, or *www.careerbuilder.com.*

My notes:

December 15

It is important to take every factor into consideration when deciding on the merits of a job offer.

My notes:

December 16

Wait until you are offered a

job before you negotiate for

more money.

My notes:

December 17

Wait until you are offered a job before you negotiate for more stock options.

My notes:

December 18

Wait until you are offered a

job before you negotiate for

more vacation days.

My notes:

December 19

Do not stop job hunting just

because you had an interview.

My notes:

December 20

Just because things get

tough, do not take the first job

offer that comes your way. It

may not be in your best interest.

My notes:

December 21

Do not cancel interviews because you have a job offer. It is always better if you have a choice.

My notes:

December 22

Negotiate for more stock options.

My notes:

December 23

Negotiate for a larger bonus.

My notes:

December 24
Christmas Eve

Negotiate for more vacation time.

My notes:

December 25
Christmas

Choose a company that values you as a person and has a culture that matches what is important to you. This can contribute to your success.

My notes:

December 26
Start of Kwanzaa

Let a company know your decision on their offer sooner rather than later. This will show respect for the people who interviewed you.

My notes:

December 27

Lowering your salary re-

quirements may get you a job in

a bad economy.

My notes:

December 28

If you negotiate a higher salary up front, your raises will be higher because raises are usually based on percentages of salary.

My notes:

December 29

If you negotiate a higher salary up front, your bonuses will be higher because bonuses are usually based on percentages of salary.

My notes:

December 30

If you negotiate a higher salary up front, you may get a better salary offer in the future from another company.

My notes:

December 31
New Year's Eve

Enjoy your new position.

My notes:

About the Author

Cynthia Wright writes a career column for The Telegraph (Nashua, NH) entitled *The Wright Stuff* and is a contributing career expert to The Employment Times. She has written a syndicated column with Knight Ridder's *News2Use* feature and continues to publish her columns nationally. She has also been a featured speaker and lecturer on interviewing skills and job search strategies.

Cynthia holds a Bachelor of Science degree from Rutgers University and a Masters Certificate in Human Resources and Labor Relations from New Hampshire College (now Southern New Hampshire University).

She resides in Nashua, NH.